Journey's Guide To Online & Social Media Safety

A Parent's Guide To Goodness

By
Journey And Terrance Hutson

With
LinesToLife.Com, LLC

Journey's Guide To Online & Social Media Safety
A Parent's Guide to Goodness
Copyright© 2021
LinesToLife.Com, LLC
All rights reserved.
No part of this publication may be reproduced, distributed or transmitted in any form or by any means, including photocopying, recording or other electronic or mechanical methods, without the prior written permission of the publisher, except in the case of brief quotation embodied in reviews and certain other non-commercial uses permitted by copyright law.

ISBN:978-1-7367937-5-6

Journey's Guide
to Online & Social Media Safety

a Parent's guide to goodness

by terrance hutson

Journey's Guide To Online & Social Media Safety
By
Journey & Terrance Hutson

Table of Content

Dedication

Preface

Journey's Little Jewels...................pg1

The Theory..pg3

Privacy Is Protection.......................pg4

The Truth Is Protection...................pg6

Who's Listening................................pg9

Misinformation................................pg11

Cybercrimes......................................pg13

The Phishing Hole...........................pg15

Post Traumatic Stress.....................pg16

The Inhuman Internet....................pg18

Journey's Guide To Online & Social Media Safety
By
Journey & Terrance Hutson

Dedication

This book is dedicated to my Mother, Sister, Brother, Son, and Daughter. The inspiration and love given is the reason for these series of services. Thank you. I love you, all.

Journey's Guide To Online & Social Media Safety
By
Journey & Terrance Hutson

Preface

This Guide Is Not a, "hey, everybody be afraid." As a Father, I try to keep my Babies safe. Any parent does. The desire to protect and that duty began at their conception. It is hard, at times, to express the importance of your guardianship, to your child, verbally. You have to stand as their example. My son, TJ, is 23years old. He has gone through my gauntlet of education in logic. His level of awareness, allows me to loosen the reins, a bit. Now, with Baby-girl, it's different. At 8, Journey is very smart. Her comprehension is high, high. But the understanding it takes to go through this life, fairly, unscathed comes with more experience. It takes a trusting in listen to know the meaning of being protected. And that comes with time on Earth. My daughter had a tough time hearing me, at first. Not her fault. I was not the best role model. I've missed some of her life. All I can offer, now, is the truth. I was scared. Plus, I did not know what I was doing. In this particular situation. Sometimes, this thing, called life is tough for adults. Grownups feel overwhelmed or bombarded with multiple degrees of responsibility. One of the main ones is taking good care of our Babies. Which is, really, a theory of safety. Most of us, wish we could see and hear everything. We wish to be everywhere we need to be. Having to face the fact that we can not. Makes raising kids, scary.

Monitoring my children's lives, devices or their friends is an, ultimate, task. Being who they look towards and being afraid they won't is mental and emotional torture. Only because we don't know. That's all. To act as if we do know, might, bring resentment from our Babies. We don't want to come off overbearing. Nor too lackadaisical. The balancing acts between insuring they understand, why? Plus trying to avoid, inadvertently, hurting them? Gets tricky. Let alone, somebody or something hurting them? Whether, at home? Online? School? Or in your neighborhood? Unfortunately, we have to alert them to the, not so obvious, hazards in our surroundings. Especially, when it comes to the internet and social media. It is difficult to stay tapped in to what your children, might, be doing on their phones or computers. The images online, things to stumble up on, the language? It is a lot. Let me tell you. These new age devices and their capabilities are something else. We do have to catch up. And it's, okay. Don't trip out. You got this. And we are here to help. We will give you some scenarios, rules of thumb and useful tips to better prepare you and your child for the weird wide web. Okay? Now. Let's get ready to learn a few pointers together.

So, as a Daughter, I think my Dad be doing too much. It's like my parents are, always, telling me what to do. I feel, I know what to do. I don't need to be told, the same thing, over and over. But at the same time, I know it comes from love. My Dad says he can learn or has learned, from me. I think that's true. We have helped each other, so much, ever since he's come back into my life. I wasn't excited. At least, I didn't show it, to him. I was hurt. I did not get it. And didn't like it. He needed to feel it. But my Dad said, "Baby-girl, the past can't be the past, until, we are able to look into the future." It made so much sense. To me. And I'm 8. I am not a kid, kid. I am making good choices. Everyday. Even though, the other kids don't. They'd pick on our own classmates, if one denounced, unruly, behavior. The ridicule and judgement from the bad influences, just by us saying no, can lead to getting isolated. Or bullied. And depressed. I feel sad, when I believe I've made the best decision, for me. Then my "friends" talk crazy about me for not going along with them. I think about being or getting in trouble. I don't want to be in trouble. Plus, a lot of that stuff is stupid, to me. So, I do smart stuff. And my Dad knows.

We had a talk, one time, Pops and me. About what do I watch or what have I seen on the internet? Mostly, it's been school room zooming. Or Miraculous. But some stuff, that pop up, like, ads and new show trailers seem wrong. There's cursing, nudes, violence and other weirdness. My Mom and Dad, have set the parental guidelines, of course. Still, some of it does show up on my screen. I just turn away or go grab a snack or something. It isn't cool, feeling like you're forced to take part in images and language you don't, even, like. I can't stand bad words. We don't need them, at all. I know, baby girl. It's like, every, show gets interrupted with inappropriate ads and scenes. I see how important our guide is, now. Not all of us are okay with the lawlessness of the weird wide web. A place, where anything goes? Oh no, no, no. That is, super, scary. So, we thought, If we help one person? That one, might help someone else. Who will help another. Keeping the tradition of 'looking out for the next', going on and on.

Journey's Guide To Online & Social Media Safety
By
Journey & Terrance Hutson
Journey's Little Jewels

At first, talking about the dangers online was a little boring. It seemed unnecessary. I mean. I've, just recently, began to use a laptop on my own, kind of. And that's for school. Not entertainment. If, I used it for my enjoyment, I would play Uno or Dots and Boxes. I mean, I am a kid. I don't think the way adults do. As kids, we can't. Duh. I don't have to worry about much. I am not interested in doing so. Some kids, I know, try to dress, look, speak, and act like these celebrities, adults or web influences. I don't get it. Because I/we don't have the same lives. Or live the same ways. I go to school and come home. I am not out trying to impress the masses. My parents? Yes. My friends? Yes. But not those that could care less about me, my accomplishments or life. And that's, okay. I admitted to how much their lives can't affect/effect me. In any way. Besides getting a laugh or other entertainment. Entertainment is not real life. It isn't, even, the real lives of the people on the screen, in the scenes or in skits. So, don't get so impressed with 'stunts' that you never mind your reality. All of the dances, trends, and hot topics are there to entertain us. Nothing more. We can follow the blueprints of the entrepreneurial, creative content providing, and leadership base. Anything else is your bad.

The weird wide web promotes, unrealistic, depictions of other people's lives. Let them tell it, they are, all, living their best ones. A life with no flaws. No blemishes. Nothing but beauty and happiness. Especially, on social media sites. Everybody is so pretty and well put together. This portrayal of their 'internet' lives can make viewers think, poorly, of our 'real' lives. It will make you believe that you, may, have to keep up with the Joneses. When your financial status or life is, simply, not the same as theirs. You start to look at yourself as less and less important. This causes depression, low self esteem and other self degrading thoughts and feelings. Without help navigating the waters of social networks, a kid can get lost in the sauce. It can make you turn on yourself. Social media/internet stories and images can lead to you tearing you down or apart. Or can it? Or does it have to? I say, no. It does not. Because it is, all, in how we approach our online experiences. Before I'd blame social media for how I am impacted by what I've seen there. I'd, easily, go search for something I am interested in seeing or hearing. What if we, children and guardians, hold ourselves more accountable? Meaning, ultimately, we control what does or does not enter our worlds. With that, the 'blame' would be on us. So, become your own filter. By doing so, you will avoid the tainting capabilities of the internet.

What if we look at social media sites as motivation? Inspiration? We, only, see how good others are doing. Why not enjoy their joy? We, only see smiles. No frowns. No one posts the bad times. Not on social media. So, just, like their content and keep it moving. Understand that, "following" somebody can not be taken, literally. You don't have to mimic or try to copy the antics of an entertainer. You can be a fan without being a fanatic. It is, only, another form of entertainment. Overall, the internet is a valuable tool. We have learned how to fix, build, cook and create with it. The online educations available range from learning languages, emotional strengthening, financial security and spiritual enlightenment. We've gotten some of the best laughs, music, fashion tips and introductions to current/future stars. So, see the use, the good and the bad of this technology. It is more of a gift than a threat.

Journey's Guide To Online & Social Media Safety
By
Journey & Terrance Hutson
The Theory

The thing we set out to do with this guide, in theory, works this way. Our intent isn't to pump fear. Nor lead you to believe offering awareness is a scare tactic. We just didn't want to sit back and watch more of us turn victim. So, the theory is to offer our help. Like I said, I've been violated by fraud. It sucks. I try to keep an eye on what my kids are into or shouldn't be into. I know how tough it can get, to do so. And as a reminder, here are a few bullet points to drive things home:

- Parents, believe your child. Don't dismiss them. Speak, openly, to them about the issue(s) they mention.
- Keep personal information items in a safe place.
- Youngsters, if you're not sure? Bring things to the light. For clarity.
- Parents monitor your kids activities. With an approach of protection and comforting. Children share anything that comes off weird to you.
- Understand that there are threats online. And in life. The awareness is safety.
- Beware of malicious software. Also known as, 'malware.' Threats like viruses, worms, spyware, and adware are some ways to trick you.
- Be careful not to give your address or location.

Journey's Guide To Online & Social Media Safety
By
Journey & Terrance Hutson
Privacy Is Protection

    First. Make your best attempts to limit the personal information you share online. We don't have a clue as to what others have on their agenda. What is lurking out there? Or the reasons why, some people, target other people. A lot of us are, all-too-familiar with being victims of the bad behaviors of rotten apples. Yep. It happened to me, too. My information was stolen by a cashier. I did lose my wallet. But I would have tried to return your property, in the same condition. With its original contents. Or as I found it. I'm not a thief. They do exist, though. So, we have to be diligent regarding our safety. Scammers and schemers are, ever, present. They are hiding, among us, on the weird wide web. Fake contests are being ran, by agents of fraud. Wanting to pick us for our particulars. They can make a lie sound so good, it seems real. In this case, ask, the caller, questions like, 'how did you get my number?' 'What is the , actual, date of my, supposed, submission to the contest?' Don't offer any confirmations or denials. For each of their inquiries. Have your own. Eventually, they will get to, clearly, determine you are not going. Then, when you are sure the call is a scam. Tell them you will contact their corporate office, for now. Mention that you will, also, contact the Attorney General's office, in your state. And the Better Business Bureau, to file an official complaint. Each one is FREE. Plus, they are in place for such. You can report the offender, by phone number. I did it for my Mom. She'd been receiving calls from a bogus insurance company. Now, those calls have stopped.

    I know. You are a good person, too. Us having to consider this level of security is foreign. However alien the thinking? We can not ignore the need. Don't give them, any, ammo to use against you. Keep your treasures secret safe. Your personal information are your treasures. They include things, like, your address, phone number and social security number.

Your full name and Parents' names are pieces personal. Even the emails sent, store receipts, and the mail you've thrown in the trash, can be used to find your private info. Your birth certificate, work or student ID, all, give a bad person, enough, details to complete their criminal act. Yes. It is a, whole, crime. It will, quickly, go down. With your, unwilling, participation. All because we feel comfortable living our lives, as we do. Be comfy and stay aware. Our relaxation is a tool for them. They will make you feel at ease. Tricking you into believing everything is on the up and up. It's not. Once, your guard is down. Their antennas go up. Next, that info, gained by an unaware, you, gets utilize. Then, the damage is done to your credit and your name. Keep your treasures, secret, safe:

- If or when, possible, shred the items you are trashing.
- Keep personal information items in a safe place.
- Do not divulge, any, information to strangers.
- Do not offer you phone number, email address or pay card info to anyone.
- Stay aware of your surroundings and belongings.
- It is sad but you must have a vetting process for who enters your home.
- Parents monitor your kids activities. With an approach of protection and comforting. Children share anything that comes off weird to you.

These few suggestions should have you guys, not only, communicating, with each other. You are, also, helping your family and your information, remain safe and yours. The invaders of privacy are an ever present danger. Stay aware.

Journey's Guide To Online & Social Media Safety
By
Journey & Terrance Hutson
The Truth Is Protection

Children, adolescents, and young adults. Please. Be honest with your Guardians. I use the word "guardian" because it sends a, direct, message. It indicates a recognition of our duties. Duties, we signed up for. That signature symbolizes the vows taking to shield you from harm. The strength of that shield is gained from trust. Trust comes from the truth. The truth comes from an honest heart. Good hearts carry burdens, as well. Have you, ever, withheld info? Or were asked to keep a secret? That you weren't, necessarily, okay with? The, uneasy, feeling inside of you is the best of you wanting to reject what's NOT cool. It is natural. You have the innate ability to discern, quickly. The discomfort stays. Until, you have freed yourself of the virus. Now, recall how you felt when you were able to share the "tea"? Were you relieved? Were you glad your silence could, finally, be broken? I was. The discernment mentioned, earlier, gets stronger the more you exercise the gift. Wait, Daddy. Let me interrupt, right quick. There came a time when I was asked to keep a secret. It involved somebody getting hurt, though. I didn't want or want to see anyone in any harm. So, I told the person that told me his plan, I was willing to tell on him. I said, "if you go through with it?" I am telling." He did not. And yes, he called me names. But no one was hurt. Not, even, me or my feelings. Nor did he risk getting in trouble. That is a win. Had he chosen, otherwise? I would've reported him to the teacher. Or my Dad. It would be out of my hands, then.

That's right, Baby girl. You need to bring these types of situations to the attention of, any, authority. A teacher, staff, principal or anyone you can trust to take care of it. Like your guardian(s). Like I was saying before Journey's interjection. We are your guardians. Understand it and how it works. Whenever, it clicks, for you? You will, plainly, see how precious you are, to us. This understanding, will hold you to a duty, too. Not, so much, a task. But an obligation. As the 'guarded' you do have a responsibility. All jobs don't make money. But they do make sense. Your number one job is to tell your protectors, everything. At least, be honest when they ask you questions. Even if you don't know the answer. Truthfully, say you don't know. Your parents won't spazz out on you for your truth. We, always, want you to know how you are able to share, anything, with us. For you to choose, not to? Is disrespectful. You are not being raised to be disrespectful. You are learning the characteristics of a stand up, solid human. You are being raised to use your senses. See something? Say something. You are being raised to use the logic in awareness, carefulness, selflessness, courage, instincts, and using your commonsense.

So, youngsters. Let us know when you've been and who made you uncomfortable. Tell us who was mean. Point out who has bad energy. It will show your guardians that you do trust us. Here's a secret, for you kiddos. We get our strength from you. You, your love and trust are the reasons, we can do, almost, anything. It shows the respect you have for us. When you show us that the seeds, we've planted, are growing. We get closer to saying, 'she/he is going to be just fine.' This leads to having, more, trust in you. Which grants you more liberties. And more responsibilities. Because you've handled the job of being honest, like you should have. Now, you hear more yeses. Granting more freedoms. By bedtime, if this guide is completed and studied, you should feel how close your family ties are. A close family is a strong family. But parents. When your child is telling you a thing that is hard to swallow? The best thing you can do is become a listener. Your attentiveness is their safety. Your control is their example of how safe they are with you. These actions, by all parties, will make home life so smooth, for the unit. It will blow your minds. We have some ideas to help you stay honest:
- First, understand the importance of honesty.
- The truth does set you free. It releases tension.
- Know that you are and will be protected.

- Having or giving information does provide safety.
- Understand that there are threats online. And in life. The awareness is safety.

Journey's Guide To Online & Social Media Safety
By
Journey & Terrance Hutson
Who's Listening?

Like my Mom, always, says. "Don't tell everybody our business." Or, "don't tell everything you see." These are, still, principles in our lives. The terrible thing is that crimes are being committed, on you. By the details you gave. This has to be the lowest place you could find yourself. Without equipment to dig a tunnel. Some of the previous suggestions apply here, too. Along with two or three more. Before we touch on those. We must, first, consider who's listening? And how they are gathering, what information? Criminals have each earhole open. Waiting to receive your, beneficial, secrets. Again, these con-artist attack over the phone. By email and internet. But also, in person. The story is deep and heartfelt and unbelievable. Because you should not believe them. If you can't tell the difference between, "I can trust you" and "I want to trust you?" Go and get someone you, completely, trust. Without a doubt. To help you see clearly. Your guardian/protector will free you from stress. They will guide you to safety. They will eliminate the threat.

Sharing family business, secrets and dirty laundry is not for you to air. Our internal affairs are ours. UNLESS. You or someone you know is in danger or being abused. We must, never, allow these tragedies to grow beyond our awareness. As soon as you gain knowledge of the harm. Help get rid of it and prevent witnessing another victim. The groups or chats we enter, are some, "safe", places our private information might leak. Because we're thinking we are among 'friends'. Speaking freely in these environments doesn't, always, mean you should or can. Though, we should watch what we say, along with when and how we say it. We don't know who is listening? Nor their reasoning for tuning in. Understanding these realities, gives you, another, bit of armor to fend off the threats of the internet. This is why and how we came up with our guide. We wanted to do our part to stop others from

being a casualty of criminal acts. I'm sure other agencies are, heavy, on the case. But you can reach out to, either, my dad or someone at LinesToLife.Com and speak, directly, to an ally. Who's listening? We are:
- Remember and Reiterate the other suggestions.
- Youngsters, if you're not sure? Bring things to the light. For clarity.
- Keep family financial, personal and legal status in-house.
- Remember. You can't believe everything you hear.
- There are some stories that are, simply, lies.

Trust those, with whom, you have a good, long standing of trust. Trusting relationships must be developed, organically. If someone is being too aggressive? Or hyped up, for you to believe them? They're, probably, full of crap. I'm just saying.

Journey's Guide To Online & Social Media Safety
By
Journey & Terrance Hutson
Misinformation

Okay. I am an old man. I am, pretty, stuck in my ways. When I need information. Or I need to find something that I can't recollect off the top of the dome. I will resort to the internet. I can find out anything about anything. At any time. If I search? But how do I know I am receiving the correct info? How do I know it is the truth? To be honest, I won't. Unless, I tap into more resources. I would seek other/expert opinions. Or even, run my findings/my theories by my elders. With this practice, I can feel confident I secured the proper enlightenment. From my will to reach the facts. There is no such thing as over sure. Either you have the confidence in it or you do not. We've been more receptive to false narratives and lies. Due to how easy it is to make something believable, to fit in. Than risk ostracism. Our human need for acceptance is rooted in trustworthiness. So, a lie seems easier to go with. Until you get lost in the fib. Landing you in an isolated place, anyway. Others, rarely, have to say, '...oh nah, you can trust him.' But you do hear, very often, ' nah, he not cool. He lie too much.' The good will show and doesn't, necessarily, have to be announced. The bad is sneaky, low down or conniving. This behavior should be broadcast for, all, to know of its whereabouts. It is a danger to unsuspecting good folks.

Misinformation or misleading information is the, most, difficult threat to detect. You can not tell, right away, what is real. Or what is bogus. There is a thing called 'content injection.' Also, known as 'spoofing'. This is the act of manipulating what a user sees on a site by adding parameters to their URL. This act is a known form of attack on a website. On the surface, it may seem worth taking a listen. Plus, we want to take people at their face value. So, we give, what turns out to be nonsense, a chance. The internet has a wealth of information at our disposal. That access puts a special power, at our fingertips. A power, us as adults, hadn't fully mastered. As a child, you can't expect or be expected to have a, complete, grasp on the power. Even with researching a topic for school, you have to be mindful of the source you credit. Or jeopardize your grade due to you not confirming the details. Such is the case in my line of work. Getting and giving the right content, is crucial. Because in my attempts to share valuable data, with you. I can't afford to pass on bad intelligence. I won't survive, spiritually or financially. It's important to receive true info. To pass the, correct, particulars to your audience. Here are a few tips on retrieving the right information:

- Beware of malicious software. Also known as, 'malware.' Threats like viruses, worms, spyware, and adware are some ways to trick you.
- Don't download anything you're not sure about. Hackers gain info this way.
- Consider the source. If trusted? You should be okay with asking for clarity.
- Can you poke holes in information given? If so? Ask for clarity.
- Are you offering info that may be used against you or your parents/guardian? It called Family Affairs for a reason.

Journey's Guide To Online & Social Media Safety
By
Journey & Terrance Hutson
CyberCrimes

Of course, cybercrimes exist. Because cybercriminals do. We will list some of these crimes. Along with a few tips for prevention. And while it seems there are no 'physical' victims. These acts can destroy a family and their future. With, possible, longer lasting effects than that of an, actual, physical altercation. The spiritual damage done as a result of theft by the internet, removes a piece of trust. Now, you're leery to enjoy the, real, benefits of technology. We've mentioned quite a few things to pay attention to and to look out for. The next cyber-crimes making the list are scarier than hackers and scammers. These crimes are far more sinister. Some of these activities are, very, difficult to track the culprit. Or apprehend them.

A cyberbully uses social media and electronic messaging to tease, name call, to spread lies/rumor, or threatening harm to another. It is hard to determine why someone would harass a person, in such a manner. Regardless. We, all, know that this is not okay. Each of us have had our turns experiencing, at least, 1 or 2 bullies. We have a tendency to limit this torment to children. But adults have their own versions, also. An abusive spouse, an employer, a neighbor or a friend can be obnoxious enough to expose that character. Though, when it does happen to our children? How should we respond? What if our child is the bully? What then? Well, our family had our trials with both sides of the coin. My son, he liked to fight. So, he was perceived as an aggressor. But baby girl is shy and quiet. She is misunderstood, as timid. Through us talking about these types of things, our awareness has grown and it shows.

We have come up with some pointers regarding cybercrimes and cyberbullies:
- Never say you are home, alone.
- Never give your address or location.

- Always tell your guardian(s) about a bully.
- Parents, believe your child. Don't dismiss them. Speak, openly, to them about the issue(s) they mention.
- Never think it is okay to intrude on, impose on or invade the lives/space of others. Even, if it is happening to you.
- Have faith in the foul's ability to be fixed.

Journey's Guide To Online & Social Media Safety
By
Journey & Terrance Hutson

The Phishing Hole

Phishing is a type of social engineering where an attacker sends a fraudulent message designed to trick a human victim into revealing sensitive information to the attacker or to deploy malicious software on the victim's infrastructure like ransomware. As defined by Wikipedia. This, basically, means that fake companies with fake email addresses will contact you, via your, real, email account. Attempting to get you to divulge personal or financial information. Guess what happens when you fall for this tactic? Yep. You got it. You become another one of their victims. There is, even a way to be compromised by text and SMS messaging. So, be careful not to open or read any text messages that you didn't solicit. Or didn't request or inquire about, yourself. Journey's school money was stolen by an attack on my account. We are, mostly, writing from experiencing these crimes. Highlighting issues of this magnitude, is our attempt to help you all escape the devastation behind a villain's angles. So, be on the look out:

- Watch out for unfamiliar SMS or text messages.
- If you open the message? Do NOT click on, any, links provided, within.
- Opening them gives access to your system and your account information.
- Even your phone can be hacked and data manipulated or lost.

Journey's Guide To Online & Social Media Safety
By
Journey & Terrance Hutson
Post Traumatic Stress

We've all seen social media videos, memes and viral moments. Right? Some of them are hilarious. Some look, very, unsafe or dangerous. And others defy logic. My Dad and I were watching videos, one day. Laughing, having a grand old time. When, I asked him, "Dad, do you think they regret doing some of these things?" Her question had me thinking. We had to add it to this guide. We began writing this chapter. Posting or uploading videos can hold, so much, joy. I had the time of my life making videos, at one point. And to get it right, then editing it? Can get, very, time consuming. But worth it. If you planned it? What if you didn't plan it? What if someone else recorded you? Without your knowledge? Then, they post the footage of you, compromised? Which is when you find out it exists. What now? Can I sue? Can criminal charges be filed? Can the video be removed/deleted?

The answer is, definitely, yes, for the most part. You have to prove malicious intent, slander or defamation of character. It can be considered a "gross infringement on your privacy." However, criminal charges are harder to prosecute, with this matter. You would need to show how it falls under stalking or harassment. Whether the charges stick or not? The potential to take another creep off the streets is real. Just by filing charges. The culprit is, now, alerted to the eyes that are on their crap. They may stop from that, alone. Although, the embarrassing video has been seen. It can be, easily, removed. Plus, restrictions can be placed on the violators use and access to the benefits of the internet. But you, still, have to stay mindful of what you put out there, too. Because other people can utilize and manipulate your images and statements.

What we mean by 'post traumatic stress' should be obvious. Its meaning trickles all the way down from the amount of likes the pics you picked to post. Or lack of likes. To the negative comments, some, 'friends/followers' make on your wall. Post you posting, those results can make you feel regret, disliked, disappointment, fear or a host of other emotional traumas. Folks have been threatened. Behind pics taken with, mutual, acquaintances. Some have gotten, physically, hurt over a comment. An, unintentional, comment. Meaning, it was not supposed to offend anybody. It was just an opinion or another perspective. Offered in innocence. These kinds of responses aren't welcomed. But can and should be expected. Only because we can't ever know the triggers of another. We have no idea what will set someone off. These days, are sensitive times. The things people find unlikable or offensive, varies on a, very, wide scale. And the slope is a slippery one. Plus, not one of us can tell what someone else is going through or how it is affecting them. So, their reaction could come from their own trauma. To help you navigate around or through, any, trauma from a post, try this:

- Respect yourself, first.
- Do Not post revealing pics.
- Do Not instigate online drama or 'beefs'.
- If you are not sure your post is appropriate? Ask your guardian for their opinion.
- Guardians, when asked for your opinion? Give helpful tips on why or why not?

Journey's Guide To Online & Social Media Safety
By
Journey & Terrance Hutson
The Inhuman Internet

Okay. Here is where things get dark. The next few statements, on the topic of the internet, are going to be scary. I won't go into every insane happening, but I will touch on a couple of things, though. We've heard about the 'dark web'. It is a whole thing. I have not been in the, slightest way, curious enough to experiment. I am not a thrill seeker. My excitement comes from learning and teaching. The things I've learned about the internet made me believe this guide is needed. Guardians. Do you remember how annoying 'pop-ups' were? God with you, checking out some, "adult," entertainment. A virus was, definitely, coming after you tried it. The web has come a long way. It is, arguably, the worlds greatest tool, these days. And as with any tool, knowledge and proper usage are key. Would you use a hammer as a screwdriver? You might. If you didn't know what screwdriver was? So, you guys. Use the internet for what it is best known. Also, use it and navigate through the abyss, together.

We went back and forth on Journey's participation in this section. We decided to leave her and the grisly details out. Nevertheless, I can't help but throw, a few, disturbing and downright despicable titles at you. I am sure you are hip to online scams and hacks. This goes past the threats and breaches of an information thief. Though, uploading of brutal and bloody images is disgusting, in itself. And there are sites catering, strictly, to the anguish of others. It gets worse than that. Other platforms sell videos of children performing age inappropriate things. Forcing them to partake in adult activities. How did the perverts get to our kids? The internet. Lack of monitoring. Lack of grown folks concern and neglect. If we drop the ball on grooming our children, now. They may becomes victims later. Educating and enlightening is protection. Give an added layer to their safety by alerting or warning them about the dangers unseen.

Initially, producing the words to have that conversation may be hard to come up with. But once you've started, the words and understanding gets easier.

I am tiptoeing around, for a reason. I am attempting to ease on down to it. Because these, sadistic, acts go beyond pics and vids of kids. You know lowlifes have been targeting and stalking their next victims online, right? Of course, I have no clue on, how? My job is to tell you, 'it' is out there. 'It" is a blankity blank blank. Ya feel me? I am talking, kidnapping, human trafficking, body parts for sale, and some more crap. Heinous mentalities are using the internet as hunting grounds. The prey? Anyone. Con artists with their predatory addictions, have creative ways to make the trap sound good. Mostly, they will play on your emotions. There's a sad story given. To pull at your heartstrings for sympathy. Or your help is, drastically, needed in a bogus scenario. And because you are a kind person, you will help. Unknowingly, signing a death certificate. Once you've shown interest? Also known as, weakness. The potential to becoming victim number umpteen is imminent.

The list of vile is long. The depths of details that could come with such topics are, too, horrific to discuss. Point being. It is frightening out here. I mean, hell. You can search and click on the wrong sites and see live murders, suicides, deadly accidents, porn and a gang of other carnage. You can wormhole your way down a mine of racist rhetoric, using, any, device. Or find yourself interacting with an, unsuspected, killer. Online. The world wide web can turn into the kind of trap a spider will set. This, particular, arachnid is a predator. All predators lay out an ambushing tactic. As effectively as the ploy works. It can be defeated or avoided. How? By you and your family being careful, mindful, thoughtful and most of all, be vocal. Guardians. We've given suggestions regarding protection and prevention. Here, it continues. Do not show your fear. Only, display a sense of teaching. Teach them the reasoning behind having concern. Acknowledge the elephant(s). Talk to your children about the elephant(s) in the room. They are big, enough, (in importance) to speak on these, looming, issues. Which are the dangers on the web, the gruesome content, the ease of access to these, potential, threats and the stress related to feedback on posts. The internet, again, is a tool to utilize to gain information. It is a place to communicate and share. Nowadays, we hang out virtually. Chat rooms, podcasts and groups give us safer avenues to, still, have some sort of interaction. With corona and all. The advancement of technology is something of awe. In your respect and admiration for the gift of the information superhighway, maintain your awareness to its, possible, harm.

- Don't shy away from the importance of your concerns.
- Monitor your children's activity on their devices.
- Understand how these issues are serious.
- Teach the reasoning behind your concerns.

In Loving Memory Of

Edna Faye Thomas

Our Hearts and Minds Are Filled With All Of The Love
And Life You've Given Us.
Our Family, Your Family
Will Be Lifted Up By the Very Thought of You.
I Love You.
We Miss You. Hug Granny And Pop-paw For Us.